the
nature
of
love

A little book of akashic wisdom—written by Laura Coe;
Guided by the Akashic Records.

LAURA COE

ISBN: 978-0-578-92906-4 | Printed in the United States of America

Dedication

Thankfully, the universe spoke, and I listened.
Then love spoke, and I kept listening.

Jacqueline, with a fiery glimpse,
you ignited my soul.
Through these pages,
and your love,
I found my love,
then universal love.

Nathan,
may you never lose your connection
to the ever-present love that flows through you.
You hold the space in the center of my heart
where no one else will ever travel.

Introduction

This is a story about love. This is a story about a return to love. A return to self-love and a return to the joy that lay dormant, in need of resurrection. This is my story, told in part by me and in part by the energy that surrounds all of us. Some people may refer to that energy field as Akasha, and some may refer to it as the energy of light or source. Others may experience it as God. For me, it is less about what we call it and more about what we can do with it; how it impacts our soul's journey, our learning, and our essence.

This energy surrounds all of us and all of us can access it and do access it without awareness. It is the energy that suggests you contact a friend in need out of nowhere; it is the energy that guides your decisions – be it a call to a purpose, a love, a change of location or a change of heart.

It is that which guides us from deep within but it is not solely within. It is around; it is everywhere and it is nowhere. It is like the air. It is in my lungs and in the world, and in your lungs. It cannot be contained as one thing, and yet it is one thing: air. And that is you. You are like the air. You are nowhere and everywhere. You are in the physical, like the air comes into the lungs and is in the physical body, and you are non-physical, like the air surrounding you. And this paradox is the key to unlock your joy. It is in the knowing that we are both the physical manifestation of energy and, at the same time, the energy that surrounds us. There is then no beginning and no end to any one of us, or to anything.

This is my story. This is the story that was shared through me when I learned to connect to this energy field, as you can, as anyone can. This is my story into love, into my heart, into my true knowing of who I am. While I studied, wrote, blogged, podcasted, and taught on the true meaning of authenticity for a decade, I did not unlock the timeless nature and beauty of it until I understood the nature of our soul, our soul's journey, and the interconnected nature of all things.

I wish to take you on this journey with me, into the energy, the akasha, into the light that surrounds us and is us. I wish to take you with me on that journey so that you may too choose to unlock this field of light and join me and countless souls who have done the same. I am not a mystic and I am able to access this field of light. And so, it is my belief that the world will be a safer, happier, and a more joyous place if we can all unlock this energetic space for guidance into our potential. Most of us look to our achievements, to our relationships, to our mothers or fathers or even to a higher power source we hope surrounds us for answers. But our potential can be seen in an instant when we experience the light field that surrounds all of us.

And know it is available to all of us, and is us.

I wrote each lesson in this series to help me heal: heal my heartbreak, heal my unresolved emotions, even heal my life's melodramas. Each lesson led me one step further down my path because it was in the lessons that I moved deeper into my truth, into my authentic self, and towards my destiny. I learned we enter into divine motion, not when we achieve more, but when we unlock the next lesson in our soul's journey.

We are all able to experience ecstatic joy, and we are all the same in our desires to find love, meaning, and freedom: The freedom to be exactly who we are and where we are in every moment, despite the difficulties we may face. Because it is not in the overcoming of these difficulties that we truly experience joy, it is in the surrender that we find joy. It is in the surrender into the simplicity that we are already capable of endless love, endless joy, and endless happiness. We do not have to change, make more, do more, or be more. We can experience any state we desire, even when our surroundings suggest we should feel differently.

This is my story into the Akasha, into the light that is always ever-present. And this is a story into my heart, and the details of my journey with my soulmate. Yes, I found my soulmate in this life, and not just any soulmate, I found my twin flame. And

I, like a Hollywood movie, fell head over heels in love, as did she. And like a twin flame love can, we found that our love transcended logic, personal agendas, and just about any rationale that previously guided our decisions. We were in love and our love moved us to transform, to break down, to show up new and to decide ultimately if love would prevail.

And it was in this love that I found my way back to my truth - the truth that I am a writer. That I am a spiritual seeker. That I am on a path towards my destiny that I and only I hold the key to unlock my truth in this lifetime and lives to follow. And it was in love that I found the beauty, not of soulmate love, but of myself. And it was in love that I found that love of self was more important than any other love, any other motive, and any other agenda. As it seems that when you find love of your self, love of the person you choose to be in this lifetime, and you allow her to show up as she alone knows she is meant to, that all else fades into nothingness. It is not about fighting for your freedom to be in your truth with others, but it is about fighting for your freedom to show up to your self without hate, without fear, without arresting who you are for an idea of who you should be.

And it was in that love that I really understood how to let go. How to let love leave if it was not meant to be and flow when it is meant to. And if it is not given back, I still can give my love to myself. And if it is not taken care of, I can still love. And if I am harmed, I can always forgive, for it is in my nature to let the rivers of love continue to flow. And if I am sad or anxious or lost or lonely, I can always find my way back by knowing I am loved. I am love. We are all love. We are all made of the same fabric and just as we inhale and exhale until we take our last breath, we can allow the love within to flow just as easily.

So, I hope that you enjoy the lessons I learned and how I share them with you through the connection to the energy field of the Akasha. And more than that, I hope that you find the joy within, that you find the flow of love within you, and that you offer that love to yourself and to everyone surrounding you. And I hope that when and if that love is not reciprocated, you never stop loving yourself and others. And if you find you must walk away from love, never walk away from the love of your self. And finally, I hope you open your self to the light in whatever ways you can in all ways you can, and as often as you can.

With love,
Laura and the guided light energy of the Akasha.

the
nature
of
love

Love is a cavernous plain,

endless and abundant,

without beginning   or end.

Love flows naturally

from person   to person

when allowed to move   without interruption.

The denial of love,

the unwillingness to allow love to flow

in and out

without questioning its destination,

leaves many in a state of pain.

The mind wishes to hold love for those worthy of its forces

but in this calculation love ceases to be in

its natural state of endless movement and flow.

When love is left to flow without interruption,

it enters into every fiber of your being,

merging with all the energies of the universe which rest

both in your heart

and the hearts of all.

Imagine you sit quietly
by the side of a river in
springtime.

Imagine you gaze at this
river and notice its splashing
waters moving freely down
the riverbanks.

Imagine you see the waters

enter your field of vision and

exit with ease, with an origin

and a destiny unknown.

Imagine the sun casts its rays onto the waters and the reflections reveal the beauty of the waters as the momentum of the flow pushes the waters gracefully from side to side and downstream without care.

Imagine the heat of the sun on your back as you find yourself lost in the soft sounds and the harmony of all the nature that has connected to this river that you sit quietly by. You watch a bird swoop down and take a small sip from the flowing waters and you see the fish swimming with ease down deep within this river.

Now, imagine that this
same river that you
watch flows from the
spot that you inhabit
to the next spot where
some unknown person
also sits quietly enjoying
the energies that this
river offers. And while
you may not know who
or where this other
individual is or sits,
you imagine that there
are many such people
seated quietly up and
down this riverbank,
enjoying the ever-
flowing waters.

Now, imagine that same river flowing within you,

its origins and destiny unknown.

Imagine the river you gaze upon,

its smells,

its sounds,

its ease, and

tranquility running from the base of your spine,

up through your abdominal region,

into your heart and chest.

Imagine the water racing

with ease as it moves up higher

into your throat

and out to the sides of your neck

then into your mind,

filling your every thought with its flowing nature.

Imagine from your spine to the edges,

up and through your every cell,

you are filled with this water.

This river,

filling every cell,

is love.

The waters,

    when left undisturbed,

        move without care,

            without interruption into every part of your being,

            no spot left dry or empty

                    — nothing is devoid of love.

Imagine this river flows quietly,   always.

The riverbanks receive the waters

and those waters nourish every

plant,

animal,

life force

that runs alongside its endless,

vast,

never depleting,

eternal flowing energy.

The river of love moves through you

                              and out of you

           nourishing everything in your path.

You

radiate love

when you allow the

love to move freely, and

that *love* nourishes all that

comes into contact

with you.

Love runs up

your spine,

filling each cell,

flowing into

your heart,

up through

your throat

waiting for

the opportunity

to move out

and into the world.

The energy comes in the form of such things as

a love letter,

a loving gesture,

a smile,

a spoken sentiment.

With that movement of energy,

the river continues to flow

as it is meant to,

from deep within,

up and out

and into the world

where they meet with

the endless flowing rivers of another.

The streams of waters flow out of each person

until we are all interconnected

through love.

Each spoken word,

each heartfelt gesture

moves up and out

and is felt and

absorbed back into

the wellspring of others

and back out.

And so,

each person,

each animal,

each plant,

each living thing

is filled with the same love

and that love flows through

and out as it was

meant to be.

And you so do through the rhythm

of love.

You allow love to move freely to anything and everything it touches.

Each breath from the morning through
the night is filled with love:

The love of waking and making coffee,

the love of a kiss,

the love of a clean dish,

the love of the walk to your next destination,

the love of crossing the street,

the love of the task at hand,

the love of the complexities you face,

the love of the decisions that you have to make,

the love of the lover you come home to and

the love that is exchanged between the sheets in the darkness.

—the sweet caress, the longing,

the expression through touch and sex.

The quality of each expression is directly connected

to our innate ability

to allow love to flow up and out in full expression.

It is only when the mind interferes

that love loses its natural force.

The mind enjoys monitoring what it perceives as fear:

The fear of being hurt,

the fear of being taken for granted,

the fear of being seen as not enough,

the fear of betrayal.

These are all seen by the mind as excuses to suggest we

hide the love we naturally have within.

The mind tells us that in this choice we will be safe,

free from pain,

and wise for considering our need for safety over

the reckless loss of self

in the name of love.

The mind says that in this calculation

we will be free from pain and life will be

better,

happier,

and

more successful.

The mind says we are okay alone and need not risk pain,

or allow love to flow.

And so it monitors each interaction to determine the
quantity of love others deserve,
and it's as if something upstream has blocked the river's
momentum.

The mind considers where to allow love to flow

and where to deny it.

The mind wishes to categorize those deserving of love

and those not.

Who is loving in return does, and who is

out of accordance with love

does not deserve the love we possess.

And in that calculation,

a calculation based only on fear,

the mind determines when to

shut off the flow of the moving waters.

If the waters wish to move within you,

but you stop their natural rhythm

by allowing the mind to interfere with their flow,

it is like the air that desires to

move in and out of your lungs and cannot.

You no longer receive the oxygen of the air

when you hold your breath.

It is you who dies from suffocation.

It is you who suffers when you stop the natural flow of love,

when you attempt to control its natural rhythm

because the mind suggests that love should only

continue under the right circumstances

and for the right reasons.

So why do we choose to destroy the natural flow of love?

It is because we do not understand

the essence of the flowing waters.

When our minds—when fear—tell us to stop the flow,

we are stopping our most natural instincts,

we slow down the biorhythms,

and we interrupt the energy that must move freely.

Unlike the flow of air,

the flow of love can be interrupted by the mind,

resulting in a similar harmful effect.

When we stop the love from flowing freely,

we feel that energy trapped.

We feel it as anxiety, fear, depression

...the river deep within is not moving.

The waters are backing up

and so our souls move back and out of sight,

our love stops,

and negative, lower vibrational energy runs through.

Like water that stagnates and becomes toxic,

we too become toxic when love stops flowing.

The fresh, clean waters enjoyed by creatures

and living beings everywhere

are replaced by waters uninhabitable by any life.

Over time those waters sit and sit

and the riverbanks die off

and the once-flowing river becomes

an isolated pond without inhabitants

—as do we when the love ceases to flow.

Now imagine this is within.

The mind tells us to stop breathing, but we would never do so.

Love is like the air moving through.

It must be free to move or it becomes toxic energy, trapped.

Yet one act of love,

one gesture toward another

moves that energy again

and we move with it.

A simple smile,

a call

or a hug offered to a friend in a time of need,

all gestures of love toward another

move this energy within you.

It is not a selfless act to love.

It is natural and self-serving, like the breath moving within.

With each inhale of love into our hearts,

we nourish ourselves with love.

With each exhale of love, we release the love we have
and that is shared into the world.

Without adhering to love's desire to flow,
by choosing the messages of the mind in place of
the desires of the heart,
our lives may appear like a deep flowing river.
But with closer inspection, the river is shallow.

The waters are not flowing freely and
that is felt in a heaviness in our hearts.

Most people wish to escape from the heaviness they feel,

so they work harder,

try to feel better through pleasure or ego-serving systems,

but they do not find the joy they are searching for.

The joy they wish to feel can be found in the simplicity

that escapes humankind's recollection;

they were born to love.

They were born to be free to express this love

in all forms and in all times

without hesitation or procrastination.

And with this expression,

with this free-flowing love moving up and out,

we find beauty.

We find joy.

We find the happiness we seek.

For those who have chosen to allow the love

they have inside to move with ease

and flow naturally day-to-day,

they may find they connect in love easily and universally.

Each expression of love moves freely.

And when love is offered,

the love inside is met by the love given freely.

So, when we choose to love another and they return that love,

everything takes on an ease,

much like the ease felt when sitting quietly

next to the river in springtime.

Imagine the love flows freely,

in and out,

like the oxygen moves through your lungs.

You walk with ease as the breath of love moves

in and out of you,

as you walk in and out

of shops, restaurants, work, and life.

And in a moment,

you meet another soul who walks as freely.

And in that moment,

the two souls connect in joint purpose

to find the love they both so desire.

The soul of one speaks freely to the soul of the other.

The harmony is found in the ease of connection

because love is flowing without interruption.

A coffee is had,

a hand is easily held,

a kiss is granted,

and a night is extended without reflection

because the love moves freely

without the mind interrupting its natural flow.

The mystery of the embrace of two souls

is allowed to flourish

without interruption by the mind's agenda

—an agenda to protect this commodity

it fears will be

mistreated, misused, and mishandled.

And when the mind interrupts that flow of love,

you move from a state of love to a state of fear.

You worry about what comes around every corner.

You worry about

the next moment,

your next breath,

your next word,

your next motion.

You worry whether you will do a good job,

say the right thing,

or accomplish the goal you set out to.

You wonder if you will ever find peace,
you wonder if you will ever find sustained joy,
you wonder and wonder

until you cannot rest because
the wondering has become its own pain.

And then one day you find someone who fills your heart

with a joy,

a sense,

a desire for closeness that cannot be explained.

You wish for that person to be near,

you wish to hear their voice,

you wish to feel their presence around you.

And in an instant, you feel movement through you

that is exalting, uplifting, even exhilarating.

You wish to jump to the moon in a single bound to

express the joy in your soul.

But you do not.

You wait.

You sit with the love.

You hold the love you have

because you fear that you are not enough.

You fear that you will not have

the love you desire returned,

you fear that you will be hurt or let down;

you simply fear.

And in that fear, you look for the strength to move

through the fear to the love you wish for

but cannot embrace.

You turn to those you love for advice,

and when that does not prevail,

you may even look for a higher power

to guide you towards your destiny.

But you find that nothing answers your call

because the love you wish to embrace

does not live outside you;

it lives in your heart,

and your heart lives in fear.

So, this love sits,

    like the still waters that become toxic

      and filled with debris.

          And you lose the love you had to the ever

            present fear that has taken over.

You do not allow yourself the joy

found in the expression of love.

You only allow the fear.

      And when your love decides to leave you,

you do not release the fear

and find the love you so desire.

And when you are left with the sensation you dread,

—that you are alone

because fear has determined your path,

you find more fear.

When we love,

when we allow love to move freely

and we find the love is exchanged freely,

we enter into relation with another.

We enter into harmony and find peace in our soul.

We find the connection to our deepest self

and we connect that to the one we love who returns our love.

If the love is not returned,

we walk away in love.

If the love is returned,

we rejoice in our newfound destiny

to walk along the riverbanks with another.

Many get stuck here, in the exchange of love.

The love is conditional,

it is not released,

it is not the love of the soul.

We can only have love,

we can only experience love,

when someone decides to release that love.

And so, when you release your love

and the love from another flows freely

that energy is met in a sacred space between your hearts.

When the two rivers flow and meet and release

and the waters splash freely together and separately,

we find relationships that fulfill our hearts.

If the rivers do not move

and the waters become stagnant,

we must leave in love and find love that flows.

Love is a state.

It is an offering of the self at the highest level.

We ask back from love and we are disappointed.

We love.

We give our love.

Love comes back because someone loves and gives love.

The desire to take love back and get love creates tension.

Give love.

And receive it when it is offered.

Separate the gift of love from the offering of love.

Give love as much as you can.

It doesn't run dry.

Receive love when it is offered.

Don't judge the love you receive from anyone.

It is a gift no matter how small it may feel

or what package it comes in.

And when you struggle to give love,

know that love cannot hurt if we understand its true nature.

An offering of love feels like offering our heart.

Our hearts feel exposed and we worry that we will be hurt.

But love isn't an offering of our heart,

and pain doesn't come

because we offer it and it isn't received or valued.

Love simply flows through us if we choose to let it.

We offer love because we are here to love.

What someone does with it is not our affair.

We don't run out.

If it isn't held carefully,

that doesn't change the wellspring of love we can offer.

We watch to see what happens with our love

like it is a precious commodity that will run dry,

instead of offering it

and then letting the other person

do whatever they like with it.

It is now their gift.

They may throw it away or put it in a jar.

We have more to give, like the endless supply

of air we breathe,

so it doesn't matter.

We want to protect ourselves from pain and mortal wounds.

We don't want to get hurt physically

or be in the presence of mental madness

that causes disruption to our psyche.

And when you offer your love

to those who cannot accept it and you violate boundaries

you can still offer our love,

simply from a distance.

At times, you may find you face someone
who has not allowed the love to flow freely,
so much so that this person stands in anger,
resentments, defensiveness, or in blame
wishing to place the negative energies
trapped within upon you.

And you may feel you wish to offer a helping hand.

You may extend love, only to find no love is returned.

And when you worry you may be taken advantage of, ask:

What does that even mean?

You offer your love.

Someone doesn't use it or value it or care for it.

It is no longer yours when you give it to someone else.

It is now theirs.

The love is exhaled into the world

and new love is always returned.

Whoever inhaled the love you released

now seems to own that love,

but it's like counting molecules in the air and claiming

which ones belong to you

and which ones belong to another.

They all belong to the divine.

Air is infinite, and so is love.

They may not treat the love they received with joy or value,

but that reflects their own relationship to love.

It is not a reflection of the love you offered to them,

just a reflection of how they experience love.

If they love themselves a little,

they will accept the love you offer a little.

If they don't love themselves at all,

well then, they will throw away "your love,"

but the love you offer is not yours.

Love belongs to the universe.

It is within us; it is us;

and it will always be.

It is not my love and your love;

it is simply love.

So when you offer your love to someone,

you are only offering love.

It is everywhere.

You are not offering your love; you are offering love.

Know this and you will never

experience pain or heartache from love

because no one is rejecting your love.

They reject love because they don't love themselves.

They reject themselves because

they don't understand they are love.

They have no room for the love you offer

because they shut down their ability to bring love in.

So allow the waters to move freely

and let the love inside you release like the air you breathe.

With each breath that enters and exits,

allow love to move as freely as air

in and out of your heart.

Breathe in the love that the world has to offer

in every moment,

from the sound of a bird chirping in the distance

to the sunlight you feel on a morning walk,

and with each exhale release the love that you have in

your heart

to those you love,

to the work you perform,

to the moments of gratitude

and joy that surround you in every waking moment.

And know that with each inhale into your heart

and exhale into the world

you are connecting to the endless source of energy that exists

in every human, in every moment, and in every cell of

every living thing.

This endless resource will never dry up,

be lost, be misused, or be in vain.

Like the air you breathe,

it is there for your consumption,

endlessly and forever.

And when you allow this energy to surround your heart,

know of its eternal abundance,

and practice breathing it into your heart

and out to the world,

then you will know your fullest potential,

you will find your deepest joy,

and you will find the universe supports your every step,

your every breath,

and your every dream manifest through the light.